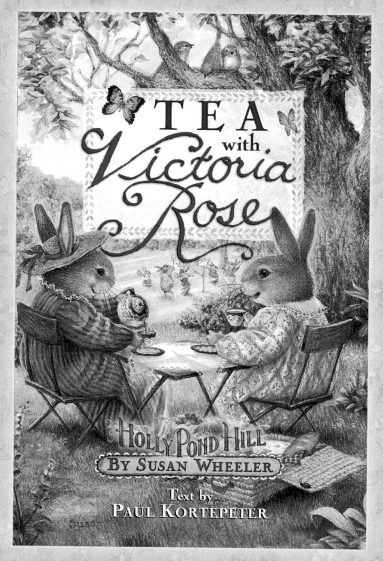

TEA
with
Victoria Rose

HOLLY POND HILL
BY SUSAN WHEELER

Text by
PAUL KORTEPETER

HARVEST HOUSE PUBLISHERS
Eugene, Oregon

Tea with Victoria Rose

Text Copyright © 2001 by Paul Kortepeter
Published by Harvest House Publishers
Eugene, OR 97402

Library of Congress Cataloging-in-Publication Data

Wheeler, Susan
    Tea with Victoria Rose / text by P. F. Kortepeter: illustrated by Susan Wheeler.
        p. cm.
    ISBN 0-7369-0511-1
    1. Cookery (Tea) 2. Tea I. Wheeler, Susan, illustrator. II. Title.

TX817.T3 K67 2001
641.6'372—dc21

00-59754

Design and production by Garborg Design Works, Minneapolis, Minnesota

Scripture quotations are from The Living Bible, copyright © 1971 owned by assignment by Illinois Regional Bank N.A. (as trustee). Used by permission of Tyndale House Publishers, Inc., Wheaton, Illinois 60189. All rights reserved.

Printed in the United States of America.

01 02 03 04 05 06 07 08 09 10 / IP / 10 9 8 7 6 5 4 3 2 1

Sue's Dedication

To my sweet gifts from heaven, Kelly, Amy, Travis, and Kevin

For all the happy cups of tea we've shared together—I love you.

—Mom

Paul's Dedication

To my wife, Jenny

"...Leave a kiss but in the cup

And I'll not look for tea."

Contents

INTRODUCTION

The Perfect Tea Weather

There is no season such delight can bring
As summer, autumn, winter, and the spring.

—WILLIAM BROWNE

I am awfully fond of bad weather. When the morning is chill and the sky is charcoal gray, when the splash of raindrops on the windowpanes makes me shiver, when the world outside blows and drips dolefully, I am cheered by the thought of tea. You see, rainy days are my favorite tea weather. The moment the kettle pipes on the stove, a sense of well-being overtakes me, a delicious feeling of comfort and calm.

Few things are as disagreeable to rabbits as cold wet fur. Nothing makes us so cranky as a day that drizzles without end. And yet, the feeling of being snug indoors is not possible without raw weather outdoors. It's the contrast of warmth and chill, of light and dark, that makes rainy days extraordinary.

With teacup in hand, I recline under a blanket in the bay window. The colder the day, the closer I hold the cup. How I enjoy watching the reddish-amber liquor bloom in the hot water. The wisps of steam remind me of the most delicate lace.

As the tea leaves steep, a sense of cheer spreads in the air. I don't miss the sun half so much on a rainy day as I would without tea. A hot cup of tea is like a ray of sunshine that sneaks through the clouds. I suppose that's what I like most about tea, the good cheer it unlocks even on the darkest day. To brighten, to awaken, to encourage—these are just a few of tea's gifts.

Sometimes I'll crack the window open to listen to the dripping leaves. Every tree makes sweet music in wet weather. The oak is mellow and stately, its branches barely stirring in the breeze; the white pine is brisk and shimmery, needles dancing like a dulcimer in the raindrops. My favorite music is made by the cottonwood. With its slender twigs and delicate leaves, it mingles wind and wood like a flute.

Your favorite tea weather may be different than mine. Tea holds a special charm in any weather, for every season. Come the spring, with her flowers and rainbows, the teakettle sings like a nesting bird. Your tea can be as green as the most verdant willow.

When the summer sun burns tirelessly in the sky, and heat and humidity are our daily portion, a tall glass of iced tea cools like a fountain in the desert. Let the tea flow freely and tempers will calm, wilted spirits will revive.

Come the fall, with her giddy breezes and tiptoeing frost, the teakettle

whistles on the stove like wind in the
sheaves. The amber elixir is as bright
and cheery as the oranges and golds in
the trees, when every leaf is a flower.

And, of course, winter! Winter is
the most obvious tea season. A pot
will help to warm a room and thaw
out spirits. The smell of spiced tea is
as much a part of the air of Christmas
as evergreens and scented candles.
I can no more imagine winter without
tea than I can imagine my bed
without a comforter.

We are often heedless of other
beverages—water or orange juice or
soda pop—but rarely with tea. It is
more than a mere beverage. It is like a
liquid book of days. With tea we mark
the changing seasons, the growth of
friendships, the passage of our lives.
And I have found that the moments
I take for tea are almost always trans-
formed. They become more lovely,
more memorable, more sweet.

Victoria Rose

Spring

GLORIOUS
GREEN

Spring unlocks the flowers to paint the laughing soil.
—REGINALD HEBER

There is no time
Like spring
When life's alive
In everything.
—CHRISTINA ROSSETTI

Green is the soul of spring. Summer may be dappled with yellow, autumn with orange and winter with white, but spring is drenched with the color green.

I especially enjoy green tea in the springtime. This bright, delicate tea has an aroma that reminds me of dew on clover. It has a taste that is light and soothing so like the vernal sunshine. And when green tea is perfumed with jasmine, orange or rose blossoms, the whole essence of spring seems to be dissolved in my cup.

There isn't just one green tea, but literally hundreds of varieties. It is quite dizzying to think of the vast selection, even to rabbits who have more words to express the color green than hairs on their heads. We have twenty different words for shades of chartreuse alone.

As a youngster, I believed that tea was a simple thing. Tea was tea and that was that. For many folks tea *can* be simple—the same blend, the same brew—as familiar and reliable as dandelions or violets. But for me now, tea is like the tulip. With tulips, the possibilities for sizes, colors, streaks and frills seem endless, bursting in every bloom. Likewise for tea.

My first glimpse of the intricacies of tea came during an outing with my mother to Holly Pond Hill's teahouse. Back then, the walls of the Tea Cozy were lined with caddies from all over the world. We took a table next to the window and I studiously opened the menu. What took me by surprise was the short list of food and the very long list of teas. Exotic names leapt from the page, names like Precious Eyebrow, Dragon's Well, Jeweled Cloud, Silver Needles, Noble Beauty, Spring Jade and White Peony. And there were all kinds of flavored teas: strawberry, vanilla, chocolate, cinnamon and Earl Grey, to name just a few.

The owner of the Tea Cozy, a portly gopher by the name of Burrows, came to take our order. He had the curious habit of greeting all of his customers with quotations from Shakespeare.

"Bid me discourse, I will enchant
    thine ear,
  Or like a fairy, trip upon the green,
  Or like a nymph, with long
    dishevelled hair
  Dance on the sands, and yet no
    footing seen."

"Yes, indeed," my mother said.
"Good morning, Mr. Burrows."
"Good morning, Mrs. Fernhopper.
A cup of ginger peach green, I suppose?"

"Yes, please. With a scone and ginger peach jam to match."

"Very good. And you, my little lady bright? What is your heart's desire?"

Well, I was speechless. My eyes darted about the menu from one bewildering name to the other, from Orange Pekoe to Russian Caravan to Sencha. At last, my eyes came to rest on a name that made sense to a little girl. "Water Fairy," I blurted. "And a cherry tart."

"Wonderful," said Mr. Burrows. "How far that little candle throws her beams! So shines a goodly girl in a naughty world." And with that, he was off to tend to the kettle.

Well, that day I drank my first cup of green tea. Even though I added too much sugar (four lumps, I think), it was delicious. Water fairies *did*

seem to dance in the steam. And the color of green against the white porcelain glistened like peridot. That day, I resolved to learn all there was to know about tea.

Little did I dream the impossibility of the task! The more I discovered about tea, the more I found there was to discover. No beverage has so inspired the imagination of entire civilizations. Coffee and chocolate are certainly wonderful, but they must forever carry tea's silken train, ever the bridesmaids and never the bride. Mice wax eloquent about pecan punch, birds sing the praises of bayberry juice and squirrels adore their acorn ale, but all creatures enjoy the singular pleasures of tea.

Tea has a long history,

possibly five thousand years in the making. Ever since its fortuitous discovery in China, tea has been prized both as a medicine and a beverage, so much so that it has been the making and undoing of kings and empires.

Along the way, thousands of writers and poets have heaped praises on tea, now portraying it as a beautiful lady and again comparing it to dew from heaven. Tea has also served as the muse for incredible decorative arts: porcelain, lace, silverware and furniture. Many cultures contain elaborate tea rituals, some religious, some purely social, but everywhere in the world tea receives a special place of honor.

Some tantalizing medical reports now suggest that the ancients were correct about tea's healthful benefits. Especially promising is green tea, which apparently guards against infection, prevents tooth decay, and lowers the risk of cancer and heart disease. Other studies claim that green tea aids in digestion and strengthens the immune system.

My Aunt Drusilla Harebell, who jumped a full row of cabbages on her ninetieth birthday, credits her longevity to green tea. Remarkably, she has managed to keep a full set of incisors.

I was taking tea with Auntie on the roof of her tree-stump cottage not long ago. Her neighbor, a frightful busybody, dropped by to scold her for drinking her fifth cup.

"This is my sixth cup," Auntie protested. "Honestly, Mrs. Beeton, when it comes to spying, you seem to be slipping."

"You know I watch you for your

> And I who always keep
> the golden mean,
> Have just declined my
> seventh cup of green.
> —HARTLEY COLERIDGE

own good," Mrs. Beeton sniffed. She turned to me to enlist my help. "I tell her all the time, strong green tea should never be partaken of too freely. It will be the death of her."

"For shame, Auntie," I said with a wink. "I've heard that green tea is a slow poison."

"Yes, it must be," Auntie replied. "I've been drinking it for ninety years and I'm not dead yet." She offered the empty chair next to her. "Please, Mrs. Beeton, won't you join us for scones?"

"Oh, yes, thank you. With extra butter and clotted cream if you please."

Besides promoting wellness, another reason to love green tea is the scanty amount of caffeine per cup. Green tea possesses only one-third of the caffeine found in black tea. Thus it gently increases alertness without the attendant jitters of stronger caffeinated beverages.

For me, green tea provides a happy contradiction. It calms me down without drowsiness. It sharpens my senses without disquiet. I find it to be the ideal companion to reading or painting, quilting or practicing the piano, anything that requires serenity of concentration.

As the springtime world awakens to the warmth of the sun, and the green of life spreads from branch to branch, I am glad to rise each morning to green tea in my cup. I do heartily agree with Mr. Sidney Smith when he wrote, "Thank God for tea! What would the world do without tea? How did it exist? I am glad I was not born before tea." Spring is filled with old delights, waiting to be discovered afresh. Like a crocus emerging from the snow, so too is the perennial delight of green tea.

POLITE SOCIETY

by Primrose Lapin

Dear Primrose,

I have just discovered a wonderful novelty called the teabag. Have you heard of it? One simply dips the bag, which is filled with tiny tea leaves, into hot water. Almost instantly the tea seems ready to drink. There's no mess of loose tea leaves to clean up afterwards, no straining and no tea ball to shake out. Are you as excited as I am about this new invention?

Sincerely,
Much Delighted

Dear Much Deluded,

Not all excitement is a happy experience. "Almost instantly," you write, "the tea seems ready to drink." *Seems* is the operative word. Do not actually drink the brew or you will be sorry.

During the processing of tea, from withering to rolling to fermentation and finally to firing, tiny pieces of leaf break off. These tiny pieces, known as dust or fannings, are gathered together for use in teabags. The problem with dust is the rapid infusion that so amuses you. The speedier the infusion, the speedier the dispersal of undesirable, bitter tastes in the hot water. Just as you would avoid the roots of a broccoli plant, so too there are some flavors locked in tea leaves that you will wish to avoid also.

Oh, but there's more! The volatile oils of tea, which are responsible for its exquisite flavor, are more rapidly depleted from the leaf dust in your bags. In short, the taste vanishes.

Tea was never meant to be crammed into tiny bags. Trust no novelty, however convenient, unless it is at least as old as your mother. Tea is best made the old-fashioned way, loose, with plenty of elbowroom.

Yours meticulously,
Primrose Lapin

Oliver's Poetry
C O R N E R

Rain, rain don't go away,
I love the sky all dark and gray,
It's fun to hear the raindrops play,
Rain, rain don't go away.

Rain, rain stay awhile,
When you pour it makes me smile,
Make my creek the river Nile,
Rain, rain stay awhile.

SPRING
SERENADE

The best music for hot tea is subtle, like tea itself. Solo piano, chamber music, brass ensembles and Renaissance instrumentals are the perfect companions of tea. Look for serenades, nocturnes, impromptus and sonatas.

Soft music is especially appropriate for gathering of friends. It provides a lovely background for the joyful notes of conversation.

Nothing captures the vividness of spring like the piano. There is a primal feel to the piano's range, like sunlight on the upper end and thunder on the lower end. The piano evokes such colors and emotions it is almost a full orchestra in a single housing. Here are some of my teatime favorites.

- **Debussy**, *Reverie: Plays like a sweet memory, long lost but now recalled.*
- **Beethoven**, *Adagio Grazioso from Piano Sonata No. 16 in G, Op. 31, No. 1: Reminds me of a long, happy conversation between close confidants.*
- **Mozart**, *Piano Concerto No. 23 in A major, K. 488: Bright and sunny like a morning amble, not a care in the world.*
- **Rachmaninoff**, *Prelude in G, Op. 32, No. 5: Silky, like raindrops on a glassy pond.*
- **Tchaikovsky**, *Barcarole: Barcaroles are the love songs of Venetian gondoliers. This beauty is the perfect accompaniment to a sweetheart tea. Pair it with Chopin's Barcarole in F-sharp major, Op. 60.*

POINTERS FOR BREWING THE PERFECT POT

It's an old-fashioned formula, but it works like a charm.

- Start with water that tastes good. Avoid chlorinated tap water.
- Bring your kettle to boil.
- Warm the teapot with a splash of boiling water, then pour the water away. This first water primes the porcelain, ensuring a proper temperature for the infusion to follow.
- Add one teaspoonful of loose tea for every cup of water, plus "one for the pot." A stainless steel tea ball works wonders if you want to avoid the step of straining. Allow plenty of

room for the tea leaves to expand within the ball.

- Add boiling hot water to black and oolong teas; almost boiling water to green teas. Green teas will taste slightly bitter if the water is too hot.
- Let the leaves steep for 3 to 4 minutes, depending on the type of tea. In general, green teas take less time and black teas take slightly more. The longer the steeping, the stronger the brew.
- Voilà! The perfect pot.

DECAFFEINATING YOUR TEA

The typical cup of black tea contains 45 to 55 milligrams of caffeine, less than half the caffeine in a cup of coffee. Green tea contains only one third as much caffeine as black tea or roughly 17 milligrams, making green the tea of choice for caffeine-sensitive individuals. For anyone wanting to reduce the effects of caffeine, here is a simple method for decaffeinating tea at home.

- Most caffeine (80 percent) is removed from the tea during the first 30 seconds of steeping in hot water, while the flavor and color is mostly retained. Watch the clock, then throw away the first dousing of hot water.
- Add fresh hot water to the leaves and brew for the usual 3 to 4 minutes.

SHADES OF GREEN

O that the beautiful time of young love
Could remain green forever.

—FRIEDRICH VON SCHILLER

Just as hope springs eternal, so does my love for green tea. If you are willing to experiment with your tea, you will discover enchanting tastes never before imagined. Here are some of my favorites.

FROG COOLER – Pour chilled green tea over ginger ale ice cubes. Yum!

GRASSHOPPER TEA – Brew a handful of fresh spearmint leaves in your pot of green tea. Serve sweetened, hot or iced.

GREEN TEA SHAKE – Blend six scoops of vanilla ice cream with 1 cup strong green tea, already cooled and sweetened. Add a pinch of lemon zest and a dash of ground nutmeg.

GREEN APPLE SPARKLER – For every cup of chilled, sweetened green tea, add half cups of apple juice (preferably Granny Smith) and sparkling water. Serve with crushed ice.

BANANA PEACH GREEN TEA SMOOTHIE – Blend 1 frozen, peeled banana and 1/2 cup frozen peaches with 1/2 cup cold, peach-flavored green tea (brewed double strength) and 1/2 cup vanilla soy milk. Sweeten to taste. Oo la la!

A STRAWBERRY TEA PARTY

Late spring is strawberry season. During the month of May, strawberry festivals crop up on village greens everywhere.

What better way to celebrate the abundance of these favorite berries than with a tea party? Strawberry shortcake is the classic, but don't stop there!

As with any occasion centered on a particular flavor, be sure to provide contrasting tastes. Strawberries are particularly good with egg salad sandwiches and spinach salad.

STRAWBERRY KISSES

These stuffed strawberries are almost as nice as a kiss on the lips!

18 large, red-ripe strawberries
3/4 cup whipped cream cheese
2 tablespoons finely chopped
walnuts or pecans
1 1/2 teaspoons confectioners' sugar
1/2 teaspoon milk
1/2 teaspoon orange juice
concentrate

- Prepare the berries for stuffing by cutting a thin slice from the stem end and stand upright. Slice off 1/4 inch of the berry tip and reserve tips. Scoop out half of the pulp from each berry, taking care not to damage strawberry shells.
- Stir pulp into cream cheese, along with walnuts, sugar, milk and orange juice concentrate.
- Using a decorating bag, pipe mixture into the strawberry shells.
- Top with reserved strawberry tips.
- Display berries upright on the flat stem ends.

STRAWBERRY SQUARES

A nutty shortbread taste with strawberry appeal. For a different twist, substitute raspberry or cherry preserves.

1 1/2 sticks softened, unsalted butter
1 1/2 cups sugar
1 1/2 cups all-purpose flour
2 eggs
1 cup strawberry preserves
1 cup chopped pecans
1/2 cup shredded coconut

- Preheat oven to 350° F.
- Separate egg yolks and whites, reserving both.
- Using an electric mixer, beat the softened butter and 1 cup sugar until fluffy. Beat in egg yolks and gradually add flour.
- To form the shortbread layer, spread the mixture evenly into an ungreased 13 x 9 x 2-inch pan. Bake for 25 minutes.
- Cool slightly. Top with strawberry jam and a sprinkling of coconut.
- To form the meringue layer, beat the egg whites and gradually add remaining 1/2 cup sugar. When soft peaks form, fold in nuts.
- Spread the meringue over the shortbread layer and bake at 350° until light brown (approximately 12 minutes).
- Chill and cut into squares.

STRAWBERRY MUFFINS

It's the cornmeal that gives these strawberry muffins a scrumptious texture. Fresh strawberries taste best, but frozen strawberries will do just fine.

2 cups all-purpose flour
1 cup cornmeal

1/2 cup brown sugar

3 teaspoons baking powder

1 teaspoon baking soda

1/4 teaspoon salt

2 large eggs

1 cup milk

1/2 cup butter, melted

1 cup fresh strawberries, sliced

- Preheat oven to 375° F.
- In a medium bowl, combine dry ingredients and mix well.
- In another medium bowl beat eggs. Mix in milk, butter and strawberries with a fork.
- Add the liquid ingredients to the dry ingredients all at once and stir until just mixed. Do not overmix.
- Spoon batter into paper-lined muffin tins. Bake for about 20 minutes or until golden brown.

Summer

ICED TEA

Summer afternoon—summer afternoon;
to me those have always been the two most
beautiful words in the English language.

—HENRY JAMES

That beautiful season the Summer!
Filled was the air with a dreamy
and magical light;
and the landscape
Lay as if new created in all
the freshness of childhood.

—HENRY WADSWORTH LONGFELLOW

Summer is the social season on Holly Pond Hill. As the sun drifts leisurely across the sky, too lazy to set, every creature is busy devising amusements to fill the daylight hours. The damselflies dance with dragonflies at cattail proms, the frogs sing together in lily-pad quartets, and the nightingales host twilight musicals. Along the Holly River, the Promenade bustles with strolling couples, some carrying waffle cones, others chocolate-dipped carrots. Diners pack the café tables outdoors, gondolas ply the firefly-flecked water, and treehouse balconies buzz with gramophones and small talk.

Perhaps picnicking is the most cherished summer pastime. On sunny days, the banks of Holly Pond are dotted with bright blankets and parasols. Picnic baskets are laden with

baguettes and Brie, grapes and pears. In the shade of spreading trees, badminton nets stand ready to catch shuttlecocks. It is a great relief to be outdoors, away from the stifling heat of houses. Best of all, the iced tea flows freely.

Iced tea! Nothing is half so refreshing as a glass of black tea piled high with ice! More than a quencher of thirst, it is a tamer of tempers, a lifter of lethargy, and a brightener of smiles. It is a taste of winter's chill, magically trapped in midsummer's glass.

Not surprisingly, iced tea has a short history compared to hot tea. It wasn't created until the St. Louis World's Fair in 1904. As the story goes, a tea promoter by the name of Richard Blechynden was having trouble selling hot tea in the middle of a blistering heat wave. When the temperature climbed above 100 degrees, Blechynden

despaired of moving a single cup. Then came the stroke of genius! Why not pour tea over ice and serve it like lemonade, cold enough to banish the heat? The idea was a huge success and caused a stampede on the tea tent. Iced tea has been an American favorite ever since. No picnic is complete without it.

I suppose the casual experience of a picnic tea is the very thing that makes it so endearing. Tea al fresco—in the fresh air. Nature bestows upon us surroundings that can never be matched by interior design. No lighting is ever quite so glorious as the sun; no carpet is quite so delightful as the grass. And somehow everything tastes better in the open air.

My favorite partner for picnic tea is Elizabeth Stubblefield. Our friendship has grown deeper and dearer as a result of our sundry excursions outdoors. We especially enjoy reading aloud to one

another. I love poetry and she loves prose, so we divide our time between Wordsworth and Austen, Tennyson and Tolstoy.

Depending on our mood, we'll set up a table on the Village Green. Or we'll picnic on the ground, reclining against the broad trunk of an old chestnut tree.

Or we'll launch a rowboat and picnic in the middle of Holly Pond. The only constant is iced tea. Tea is adaptable to every setting, so long as loveliness is there.

Not long ago, Elizabeth and I were drifting across the pond, engrossed in a mystery novel. The rumbling of my tummy kept coinciding with the thunder from a suspenseful scene in the story.

"The butler was a menacing presence, even at his most servile," Elizabeth was reading. "The storm was a source of great amusement to him and he chuckled darkly each time the tree branches clawed the side of the house. Stepping out of the flashing shadows of the study, he said ominously…. Would you like a cucumber sandwich or a

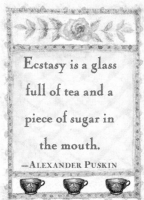

Ecstasy is a glass full of tea and a piece of sugar in the mouth.
—ALEXANDER PUSKIN

lemon poppyseed muffin?"

"How odd," I said. "Not exactly the most terrifying threat I've ever heard. Do you suppose he poisoned the sandwiches?"

"No, no," Elizabeth said. "I was asking if you wanted some food."

"Yes, please," I said. "All this skullduggery is making me hungry."

Elizabeth opened the lid of the picnic basket. Instantly she recoiled. "Worms and flies!" she gasped. "This isn't our picnic basket. This is your husband Edmund's tackle basket!"

"The butler switched our lunch!"

Elizabeth laughed, "We launched the wrong boat!"

"Tell me, please, that we still have the jug of tea."

"Here it is…. Yes, we can still navigate."

"What a relief," I sighed.

And so there we were, able to drift for another hour while the suspects in our mystery novel dropped like flies. Even the wrong boat can be loads of fun when you're in it with a good friend.

During the summer, I love to gather good friends together for croquet. A croquet tea is the easiest party in the world to host and so very Victorian! When the day is clear and the breeze is mild, I set up wickets on the lawn. Then, in a shady nook, I cover a picnic table with white linen.

I ask my friends to bring a quart of their favorite iced tea (almost invariably, Hannah Nibbler brings maple crème iced tea and Elizabeth Stubblefield brings spiced apple tea) and any finger food they might fancy. To the winner of the croquet game goes a pretty vase and cut flowers, or a teacup and saucer. My children adore this type of tea party,

only they prefer to win a helium balloon or a goldfish in a bowl. As the hostess, of course, I never allow myself to win the prize.

When the first frosty days of autumn do finally arrive, it is with a blessed sense of relief. The spell of heat is broken and the air tingles with fresh-ness. And yet, I always take leave of the summer with pangs of regret. Summer is the season from which I have many of my fondest memories. It is the season when I feel most alive.

HOLLY POND HILL
GAZETTE

POLITE SOCIETY

by Primrose Lapin

Dear Primrose,

I was picnicking with my friends, happily gulping my tea, when I noticed a drowned fly bobbing around the ice! Rather than embarrass my hostess, however, I kept drinking and swallowed the fly. Was I correct to make such a sacrifice? Is there a polite way to extricate dead bugs?

Sincerely, No Picnic

Dear Me!!

For those gentlerabbits who are inclined to fits of fainting, pray discontinue reading.

Today's column must regrettably deal with shocking and indelicate matters.

We should never gulp anything, should we? One of the reasons we eat and drink judiciously is because we never know what horrors might be lurking in our food. Happily there is a polite way to do everything. That includes the removal of unwanted bugs.

The first rule is, don't panic. It is highly unlikely that a dead insect carries a dread disease. If you notice the offending object before it goes into your mouth, simply remove it and continue eating without skipping a beat. If you are revolted or if the food is spoiled, leave the dish or drink untouched. In a restaurant you are entitled to ask for a replacement, but in a private home avoid embarrassing the hostess by calling attention to the offending substance.

Things get more tricky should you encounter something untoward already in your mouth. You don't have a choice really—you must remove the object. Put your fingers to your lips, or cup your hand over your mouth, and spit out the object carefully and quietly. Try to place the object in an inconspicuous corner of your plate.

My advice to avoid these unfortunate situations altogether? Always look before you leap.

Yours meticulously,
Primrose Lapin

Oliver's Poetry CORNER

If I could bottle up the sun,
I'd sure make lots of money,
Selling light to anyone,
Who likes the sky all sunny.

Ten cents a tiny beam,
Twenty cents a glimmer,
Thirty cents a shiny gleam,
Forty cents a shimmer.
Fifty cents the dawning light,
Sixty cents the morning bright,
Seventy cents the blaze of noon,
Eighty cents to see the moon.

Ninety cents for every sight,
Light all day and light all night.
Pay a dollar and this you'll get,
A fiery sun, about to set.

I'd be more rich than anyone,
If I could bottle up the sun,
But being rich is lots less fun,
Than sharing light with everyone.

SUMMERTIME CONCERT

Strings were made to serenade the summer. What could be more romantic than the sound of a Spanish guitar or an Italian violin on a hot summer's night? And when these fall silent, the music of crickets is enough to sweeten one's dreams.

How I love to see the gents strolling about Holly Pond Hill with guitars and mandolins in hand. When a damsel throws a rose from her treehouse balcony, they will stop and play her a pretty tune. How I love to see trios and quartets of ladies gracing the lawn of the village green with cellos, violas, and violins. The fireflies gather over their heads and the very air seems to glow with romance.

For summertime teas, seek out music for the solo violin, guitar, lute or cello. Chamber orchestras, or any ensemble smaller than a symphony orchestra, can also create the ideal backdrop for tea time. The soft and slow largos and andantes, found as middle movements in concertos, are often just right. Obviously, you'll want to listen to the music in advance for any undesired dissonance.

Here are some of my tea favorites.

- **J.S. Bach**, *Harpsichord Concerto in D major, BWV 1054: A composition for strings and keyboard that's too beautiful for words, sometimes thoughtful, sometimes giddy with joy.*
- **Brahms,** *Sonata in G major for piano and violin, Op. 78: Brahms composed this treasure on one of his summer idylls in the country.*
- **Paganini,** *Cantabile: The violin in this piece sings oh so sweetly.*
- **D. Scarlatti:** *Tea goes down wonderfully with Scarlatti's sonatas, many of which* have a Spanish flavor. Although the harpsichord was Scarlatti's instrument of choice, transcriptions can be found for the guitar.
- **Vivaldi,** *Concerto in G major for two mandolins, RV 532: The mandolins make for an unusual sound that is nonetheless a lovely complement to tea.*
- **Vivaldi,** *Concerto in D minor for lute and viola d'amore, RV 540: The lute and viola d'amore are gentle instruments and combine here to make a soft, intimate piece.*

ICING YOUR TEA

Here are some pointers for enjoying winter's icy blast in the middle of summer.

- For best results, choose a bold black tea like Assam, Nilgiri or Kenya.
- Brew tea to double strength. The more concentrated the liquid, the more it will stand up to dilution by ice. Try one teabag or teaspoon of loose tea for every 1/2 cup of water.
- While the water is still warm, stir in sugar or honey to taste.
- Avoid pouring hot tea over ice cubes. The dilution is instantaneous and the result is a tepid, tasteless brew.

Always chill tea before adding ice. The best way to avoid watery iced tea is to use ice cubes made from the same tea. You can also create a new refresher by cubing fruit juices such as a cranberry-raspberry cocktail. Lemonade cubes are also delicious!

HANNAH NIBBLER'S MAPLE CRÈME ICED TEA

    1 quart (4 cups) black tea, brewed double strength
    3 tablespoons pure maple syrup
    1/2 teaspoon pure vanilla extract
    1/4 teaspoon maple extract
    Sweetened condensed milk to taste

While the tea is warm, but not hot, stir in maple syrup, vanilla extract and maple extract. Chill flavored tea. When ready to serve, stir in sweetened condensed milk to taste or until the blend is sweet and cloudy. Pour over ice.

ELIZABETH STUBBLEFIELD'S SPICED APPLE TEA

1 quart (4 cups) black tea, brewed double strength

Sugar or honey to taste

2 cups apple juice

1/2 teaspoon ground cinnamon

While the tea is still hot, sweeten with sugar or honey to taste. For stronger taste use brown sugar. Stir in apple juice and ground cinnamon. Chill flavored tea. Pour over ice.

For a different taste, try this recipe with apricot nectar in the same proportions.

TEA SANDWICHES

Sandwiches are the perfect complement to tea, whether in the park or parlor. They are rugged enough to pack in a basket, along with fruit and cookies, for your afternoon excursion. Or they can be made as dainty as a hummingbird's nest to adorn your elegant afternoon tea.

• Bread is the key ingredient. Seek out breads that are tasty enough to eat unembellished. Thinly sliced sandwich bread is best. Typical grocery store fare, with few exceptions, is disappointing. Specialty bakeries now make breads worthy of eating with gusto. Although white is traditional, experiment with cracked wheat, oatmeal, dark pumpernickel, rye and multiple grains.

• A coating of mayonnaise or butter, top and bottom, will keep the bread from getting soggy. Remove crusts after the sandwich has been filled. For picnic teas, retain bread crusts for greater rustic charm. Avoid bulging and overflowing sandwiches by using only a modest amount of the filling ingredients.

- Cut each sandwich into halves. The traditional shape is the triangle, but feel free to create squares, diamonds and even hearts. A cookie cutter makes shaping easy. Different breads, with varying shades of brown, have nice eye appeal.
- Allow about five tea sandwiches for each guest.

AVOCADO SANDWICHES

AVOCADO CHEDDAR — Seal the bread with a thin spread of mayonnaise. Layer alfalfa sprouts, ripe avocado slices and medium cheddar slices.

AVOCADO CILANTRO — Mix whipped cream cheese with mild salsa to taste. Spread lightly on bread. Layer fresh cilantro leaves and slices of ripe avocado.

AVOCADO WALNUT — Stir finely chopped walnuts into whipped cream cheese and spread mixture on bread. Layer thin slices of ripe avocado and tomato.

CHEESE SANDWICHES

BRIE APRICOT — Lightly butter both slices of bread and spread with apricot preserves. Fill sandwich with a layer of thinly sliced Brie cheese.

HERB CHEESE TOMATO — Use a softened herb cream cheese or an herb Gournay cheese (like Boursin) to coat the bread. Layer thin slices of tomato and top with capers.

HERB CHEESE CANTALOUPE — Spread herb cream cheese on bread and fill with thin slices of ripe cantaloupe.

MARINATED MOZZARELLA —

Blend 1 cup olive oil, 1/2 cup balsamic vinegar, 1 tablespoon lemon juice and 1/2 teaspoon salt. Marinate mozzarella slices overnight. On a slice of Italian bread, spread garlic butter and top with thin slices of marinated cheese. Sprinkle with minced fresh parsley. Serve open-faced, cold or grilled.

SMOKED GOUDA RASPBERRY —

Lightly butter both slices of bread and spread with raspberry preserves. Fill sandwich with a layer of thinly sliced Gouda cheese.

SMOKED SALMON CREAM CHEESE — Spread cream cheese on bread. Layer thin slices of tomato and smoked salmon. Top with capers.

STILTON PEAR — Lightly butter both slices of bread. Fill with a layer of pear slices that have been dipped in vanilla, and top with crumbled Stilton cheese.

CUCUMBER SANDWICHES

CLASSIC CUCUMBER — Peel two cucumbers and slice very thin. In a bowl, toss slices with 1/2 teaspoon salt and 2 tablespoons of white vinegar. Let stand for one hour and drain well. Spread white bread with unsalted butter and a wisp of cream cheese. Layer cucumbers thinly.

CUCUMBER MINT — Prepare cucumbers as above. Mix mayonnaise with fresh minced mint and spread mixture on bread. Layer cucumbers thinly.

CUCUMBER TARRAGON —

Prepare cucumbers as above. Combine unsalted butter with fresh minced tarragon. Spread bread with tarragon butter and a thin layer of cream cheese. Layer cucumbers thinly.

OLIVE SANDWICHES

I prefer unsalted butter for these recipes because olives are already nice and salty.

OLIVE CREAM CHEESE – Mix cream cheese with finely chopped, pimento-stuffed salad olives and a splash of olive brine. Spread mixture onto lightly buttered bread.

GREEK OLIVE FETA CHEESE – In a food processor, process 1 cup pitted Kalamata olives with 1 tablespoon olive oil. Spread the olive paste onto lightly buttered bread. Sprinkle on a layer of crumbled goat cheese or feta.

EGG & TUNA SALAD

To add gusto to egg salad recipes, try mixing in fresh chopped dill. Dijon mustard spices up ordinary tuna salads.

A LEMONY TEA PARTY

Favorite fruits of every kind are available at summer markets, from watermelons and peaches to raspberries and plums. The fruit that is as bright as the summer sunshine and as zesty as a zephyr is the lemon. Here are some of my favorite lemon recipes, just perfect with a tall glass of iced tea. The centerpiece for your table can be a bowl filled with lemons and pansy blossoms.

LEMON SQUARES

Sweet, rich and gooey, these are even better the next day!

> 2 cups flour
> 1/2 cup powdered sugar
> 1 cup melted butter
> 4 eggs
> 2 cups granulated sugar
> 1 teaspoon lemon rind, finely grated
> 6 tablespoons lemon juice

> 4 teaspoons flour
> 1/2 teaspoon salt
> 1/2 teaspoon baking powder

- In a medium bowl, combine 2 cups flour, powdered sugar, and melted butter. Mix well. Press the mixture evenly into the bottom of a 9 x 13 pan. Bake at 350° F. until golden brown, 15 to 20 minutes.
- While crust is baking, prepare the topping. In a medium bowl, beat the eggs well and then mix in granulated sugar, lemon rind, and lemon juice. Set aside.
- In a small bowl, combine remaining flour, salt, and baking powder.
- Combine wet and dry ingredients. Mix thoroughly and pour on top of hot crust.
- Continue baking for another 20 to 25 minutes, until topping is set and begins to brown. Cool thoroughly and dust with powdered sugar.
- Cut into squares and enjoy.

AVOCADO GRAPEFRUIT SALAD

A refreshing, tangy salad for a hot day.
Serve well chilled.

>   Boston or Bibb lettuce
>   1 large grapefruit
>   1 large ripe avocado
>   2 tablespoons lemon juice
>   1/2 teaspoon dry mustard
>   1/4 cup olive oil
>   1 tablespoon finely chopped green
>   onions
>   1/2 teaspoon fresh minced garlic
>   Salt and ground pepper
>   4 pansy blossoms for garnish

- Cover 4 salad plates with a layer of fresh, crisp lettuce.
- Cut grapefruit into sections, removing peel and seeds.
- Peel avocado and cut it in half. Remove pit. Slice avocado into thin strips. Sprinkle 1 tablespoon of lemon over avocado slices to preserve color.
- Arrange avocado slices and grapefruit sections on lettuce. Chill.
- To make dressing, stir mustard into 1 tablespoon of lemon juice. Allow mixture to stand for five minutes. Whisk in oil, green onions, and garlic. Add salt and pepper to taste.
- Drizzle dressing over the grapefruit and avocado. Top with pansy garnish. Serve immediately.

LEMON POPPYSEED CAKE

You've heard of Death by Chocolate. This is Death by Lemon. The tangy lemon sauce is what makes this dessert so mouth-watering!

>   1 cup butter
>   1 1/2 cups sugar
>   4 egg yolks
>   1 tablespoon grated lemon rind
>   1 1/2 tablespoons fresh lemon juice
>   2 1/2 cups flour
>   1 teaspoon baking soda

2 teaspoons baking powder

1/2 teaspoon salt

1 cup buttermilk

3 tablespoons poppyseeds

1/2 teaspoon almond extract

4 egg whites, beaten stiff

- In a large bowl, combine and cream butter and sugar.
- Stir in egg yolks, lemon rind, and lemon juice. Reserve egg whites.
- Combine flour, baking soda, baking powder and salt. Mix well.
- Add dry ingredients and buttermilk to creamed mixture, followed by poppy-seeds and almond extract. Mix well.
- Using a hand mixer, beat egg whites in a small bowl until stiff peaks form. Fold egg whites into batter.
- Butter and flour ring mold. Pour batter in and bake at 350° F. for 50-60 min-utes or until inserted toothpick comes out clean.

- Allow cake to cool in pan for at least 10 minutes before turning out onto wire rack.
- Slice cake. Spoon warm lemon sauce over individual cake slices and serve immediately.

LEMON SAUCE

2 sticks butter (1 cup)

1 cup granulated sugar

1/4 cup water

1 egg, beaten well

3 tablespoons fresh lemon juice

1 tablespoon grated lemon rind

- In a medium saucepan, melt butter over medium heat.
- Add other ingredients, stirring constantly. Bring sauce to a boil.
- Remove from heat and spoon over slices of cake.

Autumn

AFTERNOON TEA

Delicious autumn! My very soul is wedded to it,
and if I were a bird I would fly about the earth
seeking the successive autumns.
—GEORGE ELIOT

You are going out for tea today,

So mind how you behave;

Let all accounts I hear of you

Be pleasant ones, I crave.

—KATE GREENAWAY

Autumn, like spring, is equal parts summer and winter shaken together. It is an in-between season with hot days and cold days and more than the usual number of perfect days.

I love the early fall for its garden abundance, for the overflow of fruits and vegetables, for the lilting butterflies and the fiery leaves. I love the late fall for the simplicity of its landscapes, for the naked trees standing on austere hills, for the heady winds and frost on the pumpkins.

Of course, autumn makes for wonderful tea weather. Tea can be as mellow as a woolen sweater or as brisk as a kite in the air. It can be as congenial as a misty morning or as crisp as a bright blue day.

Tea is one of the most rewarding ways to entertain company, iced or hot, outdoors or in. Unlike a dinner party, where the hostess barely ekes out the time for a nibble at the table, the point of a tea party is leisurely fellowship. The timing for multiple courses is rarely a worry and there aren't scads of dishes to clear. Most tea treats can be prepared well in advance of the party as they are typically served cold.

Many folks nowadays avoid hosting tea parties, which have a reputation for being fussy and formal. Of course, anything can become fussy if enough fuss is made, but the idea of a tea party is simplicity done elegantly. Or elegance done simply. In fact, tea was once routine enough to be done every afternoon.

To Anna, the seventh Duchess of Bedford, we owe a debt of gratitude for the tradition of afternoon tea. In nineteenth-century England, only two hearty meals diverted the day: breakfast at sunup and dinner after sundown. Anna complained of a "sinking feeling" toward the middle of the afternoon. She began taking tea and sweet treats—fruit tarts, cakes, shortbread and the like—to tide her over until the evening meal.

With such an influential patroness, afternoon tea became the daily practice for many a blueblood. It spread from Anna's boudoir to drawing rooms, and out into the parks and gardens of Victorian England. Queen Victoria herself enjoyed the tradition and the working classes, in adoration of their monarch, quickly followed suit.

Now is the time of the illuminated woods ... when every leaf glows like a tiny lamp.

— J. BURROUGHS

Tempting as it may be, your afternoon tea doesn't have to stand on ceremony. Call a friend and tell her you just put the kettle on. Tell her the house is in ruins, but the children are napping and it's time for tea. The point is to enjoy your company, not to keel over dead in the kitchen. As for the tea and crumpets, the flowers and oil lamps, these are merely the lubricants of conversation. Anything that becomes more important than sweet fellowship, whether lace or linen or the china itself, is pretense. How much more we enjoy life once the pretenses are discarded!

I distinctly remember my first attempt at a traditional afternoon tea, shortly after moving into Boxwood Meadows. I sent out invitations. I purchased lump sugar. I blended potpourri. I even quilted the tea

cozy. Everything was impeccable, down to the antique pink roses accenting my cream linen tablecloth. As the *piece de resistance,* I floated ten tea candles in my prized crackleware flower bowl.

Sometime in the middle of the party, as the ladies were chatting gaily, I made room on the table for a tray of watercress sandwiches. I remember thinking, "Victoria Rose, you've outdone yourself. The party's perfect. And you, my dear, shall be the toast of the town."

Thus distracted by my own genius, I must have scooted the candles too close to the baby's breath. Suddenly the centerpiece was on fire! The cream ribbons and reed basket blazed merrily while my pink roses smoked like exploding cigars. I was forced to douse the flames with the pot of tea.

Disaster averted, the flabbergasted

guests paused to catch their collective breaths. One well-meaning lady, trying to get the conversation back on track, picked up my crackleware flower bowl. "My!" she exclaimed. "What a creative use of a cuspidor."

Well, of course, I was crushed. I can laugh about it now, but for several months after torching the centerpiece I avoided formal entertaining like the plague. For me, the moral of the story is not to take myself so seriously. Beautiful settings and beautiful sensibilities are essential to our rituals of tea. And yet, the beautiful moments of sharing can be won only by a hostess who is relaxed and self-forgiving. Truly, the ornaments of a house are the friends who frequent it, and heartfelt conversation is the centerpiece.

Yet let's be merry; we'll have tea and toast;
Custards for supper, and an endless host
Of syllabubs and jellies and mince pies,
And other such ladylike luxuries.

—Percy Bysshe Shelley

HOLLY POND HILL GAZETTE

POLITE SOCIETY
by Primrose Lapin

Dear Primrose,

Recently I was invited to high tea at a friend's home, but the affair was not elegant at all. We were served dandelion pie and Cornish pastries and a strong black tea we practically chewed. I thought that high tea was supposed to be a silver-and-lace affair with lots of dainties to eat. Have I been horribly insulted? Should I end the friendship?

Sincerely,
Dazed and Confused

Dear Misguided One,

You are actually thinking of low tea, or afternoon tea, when you conjure up silver services and cucumber sandwiches. It's the fault of fashionable hotels and tea rooms that you are in this muddle. High tea sounds rather snootier than low tea, and now every boorish teamonger everywhere advertises high tea.

As a matter of fact, high tea was never meant to be a civilized affair. It was the six o'clock meal of working rabbits. Little wonder it is also called knife and fork tea.

No one quite knows how high tea got its name. The high dinner table perhaps? Or the tallish dinner menu? Or did some *wit* repeatedly say, "It's high time for tea!!"

You should be grateful, gentlerabbit, that your friend has the good sense to call her tea by its proper name. As for me, I only observe low tea. I simply can't abide any social gathering that would render useless all of my delightful porcelain, lace tablecloths and monogrammed serviettes. There is only so much time in a day. Life is short. Carpe diem. Low tea forever!

Meticulously yours,
Primrose Lapin

Oliver's Poetry CORNER

WINDY

I caught the wind in a jar,

And screwed the lid on tight.

I kept the wind beside my bed,

To hear it blow at night.

It didn't sing or whistle,

It only heaved a sigh,

And then I knew that I would

need,

To let that poor wind fly.

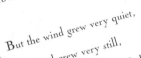

But the wind grew very quiet,

The wind grew very still,

I gave that wind a lively shake,

To see if it were ill.

I opened up my window,

I set the poor wind free,

The wind it gave a happy laugh,

And danced around a tree.

AUTUMN RHAPSODY

The breezy days of autumn find their musical reflection in the rich, breathy tones of the woodwinds. From panpipes to bassoons, this family of instruments reminds me of wind flowing through the withered grasses of summer, through Queen Anne's lace, black-eyed Susans and goldenrod, through cornstalks and haystacks, and finally rising up through the bare branches of powerful trees.

The woodwinds bring a radiance to the background of strings and harpsichord so very like the radiant sun of Indian summer. These selections are my favorites for tea in autumn.

- **Handel**, *Oboe Concerto No. 1 in B Flat, HWV 301: Blithe music, the perfect decoration for a tea party.*
- **Handel,** *Sonata in C: When played with recorder and harpsichord, Handel's sonatas transport the listener to the splendor of a Georgian drawing room.*
- **Mozart,** *Clarinet Concerto in A major, K. 622, Clarinet Quintet in A major, K. 581, and Serenade No. 10 in B-flat for clarinet (Adagio): The slow passages in these works for clarinet are so soft and lovely they quite take the breath away.*
- **Vivaldi**, *Flute Concerto No. 4 in G major, RV435: Vivaldi's flute and bassoon concertos all have merit as companions to tea, but the Concerto No. 4 for flute seems to mix best with entertaining.*

HOSTING AN AFTERNOON TEA

TEA! The word alone has the power to warm my heart and lift my spirits. No bad day can be all bad with a hot cup of tea in hand. And a wonderful, perfectly lovely day becomes still more wonderful and more lovely with tea in the afternoon. Lest the fine art of the tea party be lost, here are some classic points to follow.

Victoria Rose Boxwood cordially invites you to tea.

Tuesday the sixteenth four to six o'clock 038 North Willow Drive

Send invitations or visiting cards. Sometimes I simply call on friends and say, "Please come to tea," but a handwritten invitation on pretty paper makes the occasion more special. Four o'clock is the traditional time for tea: well past lunch, too early for supper. Late morning teas are also wonderful.

Dress elegantly, but simply. You may also want to try a costume tea party where you and your guests wear the prettiest, lacest, oldest fashioned dresses you own. Guests may wear hats, but the hostess may not.

Decorate the table with flowers, candles, lace... Use your prettiest china, your daintiest napkins. Polish your silver to perfection. Your table should be a feast for the eye.

Brew the pot of tea right at the table and always pour for your guests. On more formal occasions, serve guests both condiments and food. For the most part, I prefer to let my friends help themselves so that they feel right at home. An elegant party need not stand on ceremony.

Cream may enrich coffee, but it overwhelms tea. Provide whole milk along with sugar and slices of lemon. For a spicy touch, stud the lemon slices with cloves.

A traditional tea consists of three courses of food: sandwiches, scones and desserts. Tiny triangular sandwiches of cheese, cucumber, egg or tuna salad never fail to delight. Scones are best served with jam and whipped cream or butter. If you don't want to go to the trouble of making fancy desserts like trifle or raspberry tarts, brownies and cookies will do nicely.

Keep the pot warm under a tea cozy while you chat to your heart's content.

Your kettle should stay busy in the kitchen.

"Stands the church clock at ten to three? And is there honey still for tea?"

53

WHICH TEA?

For afternoon tea, try these favorites:

Darjeeling – Dubbed the "champagne of teas" for its effervescent taste, Darjeeling is India's best-loved black tea.

Earl Grey – This famous tea is scented with the oil of bergamot, a pear-shaped citrus fruit that grows about the Mediterranean Sea. It has a distinct flavor, conjuring up candied fruit and spice.

Formosa Oolong – These partly fermented teas have a wide range of tastes, but most are fresh and subtly sweet. They are more sensitive to oversteeping, however, so be sure to practice brewing your oolongs before company arrives.

CLASSIC SCONES

Scones are sweet biscuits. Although they contain a fair amount of butter, always serve them with butter or cold whipped cream. Most folks like strawberry jam or marmalade as well.

    2 cups all-purpose flour
    1 tablespoon baking powder
    2 tablespoons sugar
    1/4 cup (1/2 stick) cold butter
    2/3 cup cream

- Preheat oven to 475° F. Lightly butter a baking sheet.
- Sift together dry ingredients. Cut butter into dry ingredients until the mixture resembles course breadcrumbs.
- Add 1/3 cup cream and stir. Add the remaining cream a little at a time, if needed.
- Mix ingredients to form a ball. Dough should be stiff, not sticky.
- Turn dough out onto a floured surface (board) and gently knead into a round about one inch thick. Slice dough into eight equal wedges and place one inch apart on baking sheet.
- Bake 10 to 12 minutes or until golden brown. Serve hot from the oven.

Come said the wind to

the leaves one day,

Come o'er the meadows

and we will play.

Put on your dresses

scarlet and gold,

For summer is gone

and the days grow cold.

—VICTORIAN RHYME

55

AN APPLE TEA PARTY

September fruits are on the bough
And the bright apple is king of all.

King indeed! Green, gold and red, the apple is the favorite fruit of autumn. Nowadays apples are available all year long. To some degree, the apple's ability to keep, and its widespread availability, has diminished the great joy we once took in apple season.

But even so, there is nothing quite so delicious as a crisp autumn apple, fresh off the tree, perhaps dipped in rich caramel. And what about fresh apple-sauce or Dutch apple pie with cheddar cheese? Not to mention apple crisp and apple cobbler! Every fall, my family makes a tradition of visiting an orchard. We want to keep those beautiful apple days of the past alive always.

APPLE BUTTER WALNUT BREAD

A luscious spiced-apple flavor.

>   2 sticks (1 cup) melted butter
>   2 eggs
>   3/4 cup apple butter
>   2 tablespoons milk
>   1/2 cup chopped walnuts
>   1/3 cup raisins
>   2 cups self-rising flour
>   1 cup granulated sugar
>   1 1/2 teaspoons ground cinnamon

- Preheat oven to 350° F.
- In a large bowl, combine butter, eggs, apple butter and milk. Mix thoroughly. Fold in walnuts and raisins.
- In a medium bowl, sift together flour, sugar and cinnamon.
- Add dry ingredients to butter mixture until just blended. Avoid overmixing.
- Pour batter into non-stick loaf pan. Bake for approximately one hour or until loaf begins to separate from edges of pan and inserted toothpick comes out clean.
- Cool loaf in pan for 10 minutes. Dislodge from pan and finish cooling on rack.

SWISS APPLE MELT

Truly a delicious alternative to bland sandwiches.

>   1 French bread loaf (baguette)
>   1 stick butter, melted
>   2-3 cloves crushed garlic
>   1 peeled and cored apple
>   1/2 cup Swiss cheese, grated
>   1 tablespoon fresh minced basil

- Cut baguette into inch-thick slices. Toast lightly in oven.
- Stir minced garlic into warm melted butter. Let stand five minutes.
- Cut apple into 1/4-inch slices. Sauté apple slices on both sides in garlic butter.

- Brush excess garlic butter on one side of each baguette slice. Place apple slices on buttered bread.
- Mix grated Swiss cheese with fresh minced basil. Cover apple slices completely with cheese.
- Grill under medium broiler two minutes or until cheese melts.
- Serve immediately.

CINNAMON APPLE SCONES

A yummy way to get your apple a day.

  2 cups all-purpose flour
  1/4 cup granulated sugar
  2 teaspoons baking powder
  1/2 teaspoon baking soda
  1/2 teaspoon salt
  1/4 teaspoon ground cinnamon
  1/4 cup cold butter
  1 large apple, cored, peeled and
      chopped fine
  1/2 cup milk
  Extra milk
  Extra sugar
  Extra cinnamon

- Preheat oven to 425° F.
- In a large bowl, mix flour, sugar, baking powder, baking soda, salt and cinnamon. Cut in butter until crumbly. Add finely chopped apple and milk. Stir to form a soft dough.
- Turn dough out onto a lightly floured surface. Knead gently 8 to 10 times. Pat into two 6-inch circles. Place on greased baking sheet.
- Brush tops with milk, and sprinkle with sugar and cinnamon. Score each circle into 6 pie-shaped wedges.
- Bake at 425° F. for 15 minutes, or until browned and risen. Serve warm.

Winter

MERRY
MAKINGS

Tea! Thou soft, thou sober, sage and venerable liquid...

to whose glorious insipidity, I owe the happiest

moments of my life, let me fall prostrate.

—COLLEY CIBBER

Winter is on my head,
but eternal spring is
in my heart.
—Victor Hugo

As winter approaches, I spend more time watching the sky. A few late geese head south in V formation. The leaves come down in bursts of yellow and red. At night, the aurora borealis draws its shimmery curtain across the star fields of the universe. But what I am really searching for is the first snowflake. Each snowflake is a work of amazing artistry. It seems incredible to me that winter could be so extravagant with its masterpieces, showering us with millions upon millions of them.

The way folks talk about winter, it could be two different seasons instead of one. I was recently seated in the sunroom of the Tea Cozy with my friends, Mrs. Stickleback and Mrs. Chipnut. Both ladies tend to extreme outlooks and I'm rather accustomed to lively disagreements between them.

"I saw my first snowflake today," Mrs. Chipnut said, nibbling on a jelly roll.

"Yes, how glorious!" said Mrs. Stickleback. "Perhaps we saw the same one."

"The one I saw was sharp, spiny and cold," rejoined Mrs. Chipnut. "And it blew down my neck."

"Oh, dear, that does not describe the one I saw. My snowflake was light and feathery and did pirouettes in the air."

Mrs. Chipnut stared for a moment in disbelief. Then, just to be contrary, she said, "If you ask me, winter is a horrid season. It is cold, dark, interminable, and bleak."

"Really!" exclaimed Mrs. Stickleback, genuinely shocked. "I thought winter was cozy, bright, cheery, and altogether wondrous. At least the winters I've experienced."

Winter hath gladsome gardens of his own.
—DOROTHY WORDSWORTH

Ever the moderating influence, our host, Mr. Burrows, wheeled a fresh cart of pastries toward us. "How like a winter hath my absence been," he said. "What freezings have I felt, what dark days seen!"

"And what do you think of the winter, Mr. Burrows?" I asked.

"I love winter best in the middle of summer," he replied. "January is at the peak of its magic in July. A placating pastry for you ladies?"

"A mince tart please!" Mrs. Stickleback said. "And that delightful marzipan wreath."

"I don't suppose you have zucchini bread," sighed Mrs. Chipnut. "It's a shame we chipmunks haven't learned to hibernate."

Now stir the fire, and close
the shutters fast,

Let fall the curtains, wheel
the sofa round,

And, while the bubbling
and loud hissing urn

Throws up a steamy column
and the cups

That cheer but not inebri-
ate, wait on each,

So let us welcome peaceful
ev'ning in.

—WILLIAM COWPER

Both views of winter, positive and negative, have some justification. The beastly days are never quite so beastly as in winter; the beautiful days are never quite so beautiful and rare. Whether we come up with our cups half-full or half-empty depends, to a fair degree, on the way we store up memories. The more radiant the memories, the more joyful the season.

As for me, I waver between the two extremes. I'm not a cold weather creature by nature, so I need to be intentional about storing up good memories. I seek to embrace the cold and the stark beauty, rather than escape from it.

Tea is an integral part of our family's winter rituals. We breakfast with it to take the edge off the morning chill. We put the kettle on after playing in the snow. We entertain with mulled tea and tea punch and eggnog tea. Along with Samuel Johnson, we can say that our kettle scarcely has time to cool. With tea we amuse the evening, with tea we solace the midnight, and with tea we welcome the morning.

My husband, Edmund, has the temperament of a snowshoe hare. He grows more and more cheerful as the north wind gathers force, as the mercury falls, as the sky blurs with downy white, as the snow rises up around our windows. During blizzards Edmund is restrained by common sense, but if the snow comes in gently, he is outdoors in a trice.

One snowy evening last February, Edmund returned home from the doctor's office in a state of merry excitement. Stamping his feet and shaking the snow off his shoulders, he said, "The chickadees are predicting one foot, the grosbeaks are calling for 18 inches and the cardinals two entire feet!"

"So, whatever the outcome, we're in for some serious snow," I said.

"Serious!" he said happily. "Devastating! Catastrophic!" He gave me a giddy twirl around the foyer. "Dear, dear Mrs. Boxwood…"

"Yes, my love?" I could tell Edmund was up to something.

"Dear, sweet Mrs. Boxwood, my wife, my heart's delight, my apple strudel…. How would you like to go for a skate with me? Before the snow covers the ice? It is simply dreamy out there!"

"Dreamy! How can I pass up dreamy?"

And dreamy it was. All around us the trees were sugary white. The snow appeared magically out of the gray overhead and made swishes through the branches. No other sound, save the occasional note of a partridge, reached our ears. It seemed as if we were the last two rabbits on earth.

The river glistened in the half-light, a ribbon of frosty blue meandering through the forest. The only speck of warmth was a gas lamp winking stoically near the old stone bridge. The snow started falling harder and the trees behind the trees vanished in a screen of white. A shiver went down my back.

Edmund sang out, "What a pleasure it is to sally forth into this winter wonderland!"

On we skated, arm in arm. The trees sailed by and the cottages too. Although I had grown up on Holly Pond Hill, and I was sure of every twist and turn in the river, I felt as if I were breezing through an unexplored world. It was as exhilarating as sightseeing in a foreign land.

The exertion of skating warmed me for a time. It didn't take long, however, for the cold to catch up with me. I didn't really want to turn around, not with Edmund growing more and more ebullient, but my shivers were growing stronger. At last, I could bear it no longer.

"Edmund, shall we reverse direction?"

"By no means!"

"I'll make you a hot cup of tea honeyed with mead."

"Darling, your very presence warms me through and through."

"How about rum raisin muffins, fresh from the oven?"

"You are my rum raisin muffin!"

Sometimes one must spell things out very clearly to a gent. "Edmund, I am cold enough to adhere to the ice. If you have a gallant bone in your body,

you will immediately…"

But I never did finish my sentence. Up ahead, around a bend in the river, flamed a splendid bonfire. As we neared the stone circle, I could see a thermos, two mugs and a pile of woolen blankets. I was too surprised to speak.

"Hot tea, I presume?" Edmund asked.

With the blankets under me, a fire to my back and a mug of steaming tea upon my lips, I felt toasty in no time.

"Here's to the winter," Edmund said, holding up his mug.

"And to the love that keeps us warm."

We clanked our mugs together. All around the snow poured down, but for us it seemed to part above our fire.

HOLLY POND HILL
GAZETTE

POLITE SOCIETY

by Primrose Lapin

Dear Primrose,

I have always added a squeeze of lemon to my green and herbal teas. The tartness tickles my palate. At a recent soirée, however, a friend informed me that lemon was to be taken with black tea only. I am certain she is wrong, but I would like to show her your column and gloat.

Most sincerely yours,
Lemon Lover

Dear Lemon Lass,

Horrors! Lemon in green and herbal teas! There is a reason we don't add lemon to delicate teas. It completely sours the taste. Of course, if you take lemon in the privacy of your own home, it's not exactly a moral lapse. But squeezing lemon into herbal teas at a tea party is tantamount to belching.

Gentlerabbits, kindly remember these simple points of tea etiquette and you will have everyone's undying gratitude:

1. Naught should be added to green and herbal teas save the sweetener. No lemon. No milk.

2. Spread butter on the scone before adding jam. When using whipped cream, however, spread the jam on first and then the cream.

3. Even though we say "cream and sugar" at tea parties, never add real cream. Real cream swamps a good cup of tea. By cream, we mean whole milk. Save your real cream for coffee.

4. Never leave your spoon in your teacup. When accidentally hit, a spoon can act as a catapult, throwing scalding liquid across the table.

5. Avoid extending your pinky finger while sipping tea. This affectation always looks a little like rigor mortis.

Always seek to put those around you at ease. Thinking of others and caring about their feelings is the whole purpose of etiquette.

Meticulously yours,
Primrose Lapin

Oliver's Poetry CORNER

SNOWFLAKES

I'd like to frame each snowflake,
And hang them down the hall,
For each is like a work of art,
To view upon the wall.

I wouldn't need a Rembrandt,
A Picasso or Matisse,
I wouldn't need van Gogh,
To view a masterpiece.

Each snowflake is a beauty,
And each deserves a stare,
And yet I think I'd rather
Lick them in the air.

WINTER AIRS

If any form of music captures the "sound" of winter—from the festive, merry notes of Christmas to the procession of solemn days—it must be the music of the Renaissance. The instruments greet modern ears with a barrage of unusual sounds. Even the names of the instruments are strange: shawms, crumhorns, sackbuts, lutes, viols, citterns, bandoras, hurdy gurdies, and tabors.

And yet, there is something vaguely familiar about the music. Perhaps Christmas carols are the link. Caroling flowered as the Renaissance spread north. A goodly number of Christmas melodies come down to us from Renaissance minstrels: "Greensleeves" ("What Child Is This?"), "The Boar's Head," and "Ding Dong Merrily On High," to name a few.

As for music befitting social tea, look for early music consorts with a repertoire of pretty instrumentals. Renaissance music can run the gamut from sedate to raucous, but the consorts are typically sextet-sized, smaller than a chamber orchestra, hence a suitable volume. Look also for albums featuring solo lute, viol or recorder.

Don't ignore brass ensembles either! Although we associate brass instruments with pomp and parades, they have a softer side too, particularly the English and French horns. Trumpets, trombones and tubas are the most resolutely cheerful of all instruments, which is certainly needed at times during winter.

DR. BOXWOOD'S GUIDE TO SOOTHING A COLD

Dr. Edmund Boxwood at your service. Most townsfolk know me simply as "Victoria Rose's husband." When I'm not decorating my wife's arm like an overgrown corsage, I am either practicing medicine or fishing.

No cure has yet been concocted for the common cold. Once the sneezing and sore throat begin, typical cold symptoms last about four days to a week. Along the way, it's nice to know that tea can help alleviate some of the distress.

Hot black tea is the key ingredient in these recipes, not only for its soothing warmth, but also for supplying the body with much-needed liquid.

LEMON MINT TEA – To ease the pain of a sore throat, brew one cup of hot tea with five or six fresh peppermint leaves. Squeeze juice from a wedge of lemon into the infusion and add honey to taste. Strain before sipping.

CAYENNE TEA – To warm the whole body, add 1/4 teaspoon of cayenne pepper powder to 1/2 cup of milky hot tea. The feeling of well-being afterwards makes amends for the fiery sensations you'll experience.

CONGESTION KICKER – The pungent "kick" of this brew will help unstuff a stuffy nose. First, grate one tablespoon of fresh gingerroot for every cup

of water. Second, make a decoction of the ginger by simmering it for ten minutes on the stovetop. Allow to cool. Third, brew hot tea and blend it in equal parts with the ginger decoction. Strain the beverage. Lastly, add a squeeze of lemon or lime, and a sprinkling of cayenne and honey to taste.

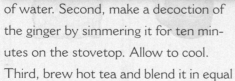

TEA
BEVERAGES

Tea adds complexity to fruit punches and holiday drinks. Its astringency gives some "kick" to drinks without overpowering them. Make sure you sample each beverage before serving so that it suits your taste. Cheers!

FRUIT BREEZE

    3 cups orange juice

    2 cups cranberry-raspberry juice
      cocktail

    2 cups raspberry-flavored black tea,
      sweetened

    2 tablespoons fresh lime juice

    3 cups lemon-lime soda

    1/2 cup frozen or fresh raspberries

    Twists of lemon and lime peel

• Chill all liquids before mixing. In a large punch bowl, combine the juices

and tea.

• Add soda, raspberries and citrus twists just before serving.

• Keep chilled with ice cubes.

ALMOND PUNCH

    3 lemons

    4 cups water

    2 cups granulated sugar

    2 cups pineapple juice

    2 cups black tea

    1 teaspoon almond extract

    1 teaspoon vanilla extract

    4 cups ginger ale, chilled

• Squeeze lemons into bowl and reserve juice.

• Place lemon rinds in a large saucepan and add sugar and water. Boil for three minutes.

- Add lemon juice, pineapple juice, almond and vanilla extracts. Strain into punch bowl and chill.
- When ready to serve, add chilled ginger ale.

HOT WASSAIL

Wet your whistle before caroling or warm your toes afterwards.

>   4 cups hot black tea
>   2 cups sugar
>   12 whole cloves
>   4 sticks cinnamon
>   2 tablespoons chopped fresh ginger
>   4 whole allspice
>   2 quarts apple cider
>   3 cups orange juice
>   2 cups lemon juice
>   2 tablespoons butter

- In a large saucepan, pour hot tea over sugar. Stir until sugar has dissolved.
- Bring the mixture to a boil and boil for

10 minutes to make sweet tea syrup. Remove from heat.

- Add cloves, cinnamon, ginger and allspice. Allow the spices to steep in the warm tea syrup for an hour.
- Strain away the spices and return clarified tea syrup to a large saucepan.
- Add cider, orange juice and lemon juice. Bring to boiling, add butter and serve in mugs.

HOT TEA EGGNOG

    1 quart sweetened black tea
    2 cups commercially prepared
      eggnog
    Fresh ground nutmeg to taste

In a saucepan, combine tea and eggnog. Stir over medium heat until the mixture is steaming. Do not boil. Serve immediately with a sprinkling of ground nutmeg.

Postscript
TEA FOR QUIET TIMES

There is a quiet side to tea.

True, tea is perfectly at home in the hurry of a workaday breakfast. It harmonizes as well with the laughter of friends as with the formalities of high society. It appears magically in the cracked cups of children playing tea party. It is drunk by hagglers at the bazaar and by honeymooners in their getaway cabins.

But there is, as I have said, a quiet side to tea. It is a side that has no need for conversation. It shuns the center of attention. It eschews anxiety. It refuses to hurry. As often as tea invites us to be social, tea calls us to time alone. Time to turn inward. Time to shut the heart from worry. Time to turn thoughts into prayers.

The telephone is ringing—let it ring. The work is piling up—let it pile. Often, nothing is more necessary than a pause for quiet. In quiet we can hear the still, small voice of God. In quiet, God often sends His best thoughts.

Sometimes I put the kettle on for me alone. While I wait for the water to boil, I read the Bible. Or I read hymns

Tea is drunk to
forget the din
of the world.
—T'IEN YIHENG

and sacred poetry. Or I simply listen to the silence. Tea helps me to listen better. It helps me to focus my attention, keeping me alert while I walk the path of prayer.

The warm presence of tea reminds me to seek the warmer presence of God's love, warmth that never grows cold. The steeping tea leaves remind me that I must immerse myself in His Word before the fruits of His Spirit can be extracted from me (Psalm 1:1-2). The delicious taste of tea reminds me to taste and see that the Lord is good (Psalm 34:8). The honey reminds me to be thankful for sweet fellowship with the Lord (Psalm 119:103).

If tea fulfills a kind of destiny, it is in the nurture of the soul during times of quiet, times of reflection, times of prayer. I have come to see tea as a keepsake of God's unfailing care, a memento of His promises.

God hath promised
Strength for the day,
Rest for the labor,
Light for the way,
Grace for the trials,
Help from above,
Unfailing sympathy,
Undying love.

—ANNIE JOHNSON FLINT

When I turn from my times of quiet, I am more certain of the vision set before me. Life can be more beautiful. Life can be more sacred. And that Life, which lives within me, helps me to live in all ways more abundantly.

Love is a fruit in season at all times, and within reach of every hand.
—MOTHER TERESA